Conor's Magical Treasure Hunt

Lady Kimberly Motes Doty

ISBN 979-8-8690-7845-2 (paperback)
ISBN 979-8-8690-7846-9 (digital)

Lady Kimberly Industries LLC
Madeira Beach, Florida 33708-9998

LadyKimberlyBooks.com
LadyKimberlyIndustries.com

Conor's Magical Treasure Hunt

Once upon a sunny day, in a small coastal town, there lived a curious and adventurous boy named Conor.

Conor loved spending time with his grandmother, Mimi, who was full of stories and wisdom.

One summer day, Conor and Mimi decided to go on a special treasure hunt on the beach. They were on a mission to find the perfect Conch shell. Conor had heard tales of its magical sound and wanted to experience it himself.

With their buckets and shovels in hand,
Conor and Mimi set off along the sandy
shore.

As they walked, they admired the sparkling waves and listened to the seagulls' cheerful songs. Conor's excitement grew with every step.

The beach was vast, filled with shells of all shapes and sizes.

Conor picked up shells one by one, examining each carefully, hoping to find the perfect Conch shell. But no matter how beautiful the shells were, none of them had the magical sound he longed for.

They continued their search, determined and hopeful. Conor's eyes sparkled with anticipation, and Mimi's smile reflected her love for her grandson's adventurous spirit.

They laughed and shared stories as they combed the beach, their bond growing stronger with every moment.

Conor and Mimi's treasure hunt on the beach was filled with excitement and joy.

As they continued their search, they encountered various sea creatures along the way.

They came across a group of playful dolphins leaping out of the water, their sleek bodies glistening in the sunlight.

Conor and Mimi stood in awe, watching the dolphins dance and play, their laughter mingling with the sound of the crashing waves.

Further along the shore, they came upon a family of curious seagulls.

The seagulls squawked and flapped their wings, seemingly interested in Conor and Mimi's treasure hunt

Conor couldn't help but toss a few crumbs their way, causing a frenzy of feathers and squawks.

As they explored the beach, Conor and Mimi discovered fascinating seashells in all colors and patterns.

Conor's bucket quickly filled with treasures, though none of them matched the beauty and magic of the Conch shell he sought.

Their journey took them to a hidden cove, where the sound of the waves was softer, and the sand was warm beneath their feet.

In this tranquil spot, Conor and Mimi sat down to rest and enjoy a picnic.

With renewed energy, they continued their search, digging deeper into the sand and examining every shell they found.

Conch shells are a threatened species now so finding one is very rare and special.

Conor's determination never wavered, and Mimi's encouragement fueled his spirit.

She shared stories of her own treasure hunts as a child, filling his imagination with tales of hidden treasures and secret caves.

As the sun began to dip below the horizon, casting a golden glow over the beach, Conor's hands finally found the perfect Conch shell.

It was a moment of pure joy and triumph. His heart skipped a beat as he carefully unearthed it.

It was the most beautiful Conch shell he had ever seen, with its swirling patterns and gentle curves.

Conor held it close, feeling the warmth of his accomplishment.

Conor held it up to his ear, and the sound that emanated from it was pure magic.

It was the sound of the sea, whispering secrets and dreams.

Conor and Mimi returned home, their hearts filled with happiness and the memory of their treasure hunt forever etched in their minds.

Conor placed the Conch shell on his bedside table, where it would serve as a reminder of their adventure and the love between him and his grandmother.

Conor and Mimi continued to explore the world, discovering new wonders and creating beautiful memories.

And whenever they needed a little magic,
they would hold the Conch shell to their
ears, listening to the whispers of the sea
and feeling the love that bound them
together

From that day on, Conor and Mimi's treasure hunt became a cherished memory, shared with friends and family.

Conor would often recount the story, inspiring other children to embark on their own adventures and treasure hunts, reminding them of the importance of perseverance, love, and the magic that lies within the simplest moments.

The End.

About the Author

Lady Kimberly Motes Doty has dedicated her life to helping people in many different ways.

She is a minister, which means she helps others find their spiritual path.

She is also a life coach, which means she guides people to live their best lives.

Lady Kimberly is even a natural health specialist, which means she knows a lot about taking care of our bodies and staying healthy. In addition to all of this, she loves to write and share her wisdom with others. When she's not working, she enjoys spending time with her family.

ladykimberlyindustries.com/

LadyKimberlyBooks

More Lady Kimberly Children's Books

Introducing children to the wonders of God and the teachings of the Bible is a vital aspect of their spiritual development. That's why "A Children's Guide to A Godly Way of Life" is the ideal resource to nurture their curiosity and guide them towards a deeper understanding of faith. By introducing them to the commandments and the valuable lessons Jesus taught us about living a godly life, we can provide them with a solid foundation in their spiritual journey.

"A Children's Guide to a Godly Way of Life" is not just another ordinary book. It is a treasure trove of knowledge and wonder, carefully crafted to quench the thirst for understanding that resides within every child's soul. With each turn of the page, their imagination will ignite, propelling them on a lifelong voyage of love and devotion to God, and an insatiable hunger for unraveling the mysteries of the divine.

"Discovering God's Love: A Magical Journey of Faith and Wonder"

Introducing a captivating new children's book series by the talented author, Lady Kimberly Motes Doty. "Discovering God's Love" is an exploration of God's love and teachings through enchanting and relatable stories that conveys the sense of curiosity and discovery that young readers will experience as they delve into each book. "Discovering God's Love" emphasizes the spiritual growth and lifelong connection with God. The first five books in the series have been released with the full series to include short stories about the commandments, how to treat others, how to treat animals, and our own personal growth with God.

This extraordinary collection aims to teach children about God's boundless love and His teachings from the Bible through enchanting short stories. Lady Doty has masterfully crafted these tales to speak directly to children in a language they can easily understand, making each book both Biblically based and effortlessly relatable.

"What or Who is God?" is a captivating children's book that follows the curious and kind-hearted girl, Aurora, on a quest to uncover the answer to a timeless question: What or who is God?

"Where is God?" is a heartwarming children's book that follows the journey of Aurora, a curious young girl, as she seeks to understand the presence of God. Wondering where God is, Aurora embarks on a quest to discover His whereabouts.

"Does God Lie?" is an enchanting tale that follows the journey of two siblings, Aurora and Cade, as they stumble upon a mysterious old book about God's promises. Intrigued by the idea of unwavering faithfulness, they embark on a quest to learn more about the reliability

of God's word.

Join Aurora, Cade, and Conor on a thrilling treasure hunt that takes them on a journey through the wonders of

God's creation in "Is Everything God Does Good?" This exciting story reminds young readers of the beauty and love found in God's creations and the importance of being good stewards of the natural world.

"What Are Angels?" is a exhilarating children's book that explores the concept of angels and their role in our lives. Through the eyes of a curious little boy named Cade, his fascination with angels leads him to ask his mother about their purpose and how they keep us safe. In response, his loving mother imparts wisdom and shares stories from the Bible. She explains that angels, although invisible to the human eye, are like invisible superheroes sent by God to watch over and protect us.

One day, while playing near a majestic oak tree, the three curious cousins Aurora, Conor and Cade happen upon a special book called the Bible. As they

open its pages, they discover the concept of commandments – rules given by God to guide them in living a purposeful and fulfilling life. Driven by their newfound understanding, Aurora, Conor, and Cade embark on a mission to put these commandments into action in their daily lives.

"Is Anger Bad?" is a charming tale that teaches children about the power of anger and how to handle it wisely. Through relatable characters and captivating storytelling, this book empowers young readers to embrace their emotions and make a positive impact on the world.

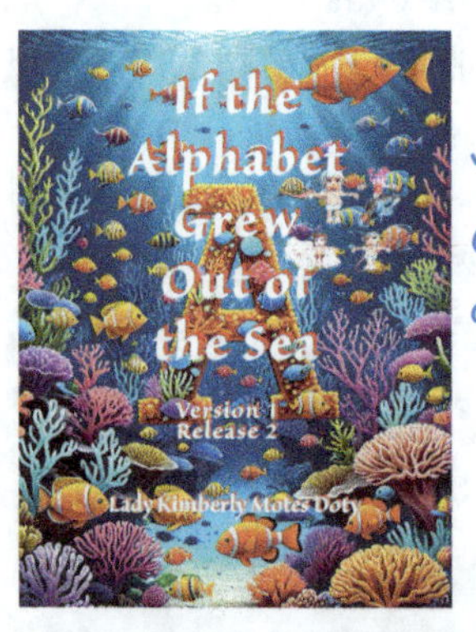

"If The Alphabet Grew Out of The Sea v2" – Almost 600 pages of mazes, word searches and fun facts about sea animals on an exciting Sea Adventure!

"If the Alphabet Grew Out of The Sea" V1 – in English, French & Spanish

www.ingramcontent.com/pod-product-compliance
Lightning Source LLC
Chambersburg PA
CBHW070327160726
47999CB00003B/1190